About The Bible

Copyright owned by
Betty Sue Tracy.
2010
All rights reserved

Christianity
PO Box 20009
Carson City, Nevada 89721
Homeschoolwwh.com
978 0 9779951 6 5

The right of reproduction of this book is reserved exclusively for the author who grants permission for brief quotes to be used for review purposes as long as full credit is given to the author.

"Thou shalt not muzzle the ox that treadeth out the corn. And, the laborer is worthy of his reward." 1 Timothy 5:18 (1 Corinthians 9:9, Deuteronomy 25:4, Luke 10:7, Matthew 10:10, Deuteronomy 24:15.)

"Therefore, behold, I am against the prophets, saith the Lord, that steal my words every one from his neighbor." Jeremiah 23:30

:...Thou shalt not steal, ... Thou shalt love thy neighbor as thyself." Romans 13:9 (Matthew 19:18, Mark 10:19, Luke 18:20, 1 Corinthians 6:8,10, Ephesians 4:28, Exodus 20:15, Leviticus 19:11,13, Deuteronomy 5:19, Leviticus 19:18, Matthew 5,:43, 7:12, 19:19, 22,:39, Mark 12:31, Luke 10:27, Galatians 5:14, James 2:8)

"Render therefore to all their dues: ... honor to whom honor." Romans 13:7

"That no man go beyond and defraud his brother in any matter: because that the Lord is the avenger of all such, as we also have forewarned you and testified." 1 Thessalonians 4:6 (Leviticus 19:13, Deuteronomy 32:35, Proverbs 22:22,23)

Scriptures compiled by the Bluedorns, Triviumpursuit.com.

Cover picture Cora Wiltse's Bible from her youth.

1. Is There A God?..3
2. Jesus Christ of Nazareth......................................7
3. The Truth Of Christian Wars And Violence........11
4. Good and Evil 19
5. The Bible..21
6. Facts About The Bible..22
7. Fun Facts...27
8. Where Did Our Bible Come From? 29
9. The English Bible...31
10. The Bible Comes of Age....................................35
11. The King James...37
12. Our Modern Versions...39
13. A Comparison..41
14. Which Bible to Use 44
15. Biblical Interpretation...47
16. The Cannon Bible..49
17. Bible Helps..53
18. Dating Creation..57
19. Can We Believe?...59

1. Is There A God?

This is the fundamental question of life on which all other questions hang. If there is no God then life has no purpose beyond our momentary pleasure. There is no meaning. There is no right or wrong. Take all you can get and enjoy yourself for the moment because when it is over, it is OVER. That is all she wrote, so to speak.

If there is a God, however, then there is a heaven to gain and a hell to shun; a Great White Throne to stand in front of and give answer to. There is a right and a wrong. There is an eternity that is more real than anything you have every experienced in your life, good or bad.

Can we know if there is a God? And if so, how?

Within the cells of every living organism is a thing called DNA. This is the programming that determines whether you are a watermelon or a woman, whether you have blue eyes or brown, whether you are tall or short. This DNA is an intricate code that we humans are just now beginning to be able to read.

Noah Webster says:
CODE,
n. Any collection or digest of laws.

LAW,
n. [L. lex; A law is that which is laid, set or fixed, like statute, constitution, from L. statuo.]
*1. A rule, particularly an established or permanent rule, prescribed by the **supreme power** of a state to its subjects, for regulating their actions, particularly their*

1. Is There a God?

social actions. Laws are imperative or mandatory, commanding what shall be done; prohibitory, restraining from what is to be forborne; or permissive, declaring what may be done without incurring a penalty. The laws which enjoin the duties of piety and morality are prescribed by God and found in the Scriptures. (Emphasis mine.)

You do not have green vines coming out of your ears, grapes hanging off your nose, or a horse-like tail because the laws prescribed by the Supreme Power who wrote your DNA says you don't.

Could your DNA have written itself?

No. DNA is a language. Language takes intelligence.

LAN'GUAGE, *n. [L. lingua, the tongue, and speech.]*

Words duly arranged in sentences, written, printed or engraved, and exhibited to the eye. (DNA is exhibited to the eye through the microscope. Different from my glasses only in degree) *Style; manner of expression. Any manner of expressing thoughts.*

"Any manner of expressing thoughts." For DNA to express thoughts there had to be thoughts to express before it was written down in our cells. There has to be a Creator God.

Have you ever examined a giraffe? Their necks are so tall they must have an extraordinarily strong heart in order to pump the blood all the way up there. But with such a strong heart, if they bend their head down, gravity + the heart would blow their brains out

1. Is There a God?

(high blood pressure). So they have a set of valves in the arteries of their necks that shut the blood flow down when they put their head down. But then when they lift their heads suddenly (as in a lion attack) they would pass out (low blood pressure). So they have little sponges in the back of their brains that hold enough blood in reserve to keep them conscious until the valves open again. If any one of these steps were missing, the giraffe would die (either by exploding brain or hungry lion). They must have all been there from the start. They could not have evolved. They must have been created as a complete animal.

There are many other creatures (the woodpecker who would knock its eyes out if it had not been programmed to close its eyes with each strike, the garden spider which would starve if its web was not just right, the chicken egg where the chick would suffocate without its microscopic air holes, the human eye, the bombardier beetle which would blow itself up if it did not have all systems functioning at once, etc.) that simply could not exist without a Divine Design[1]. There must be a God.

---

[1] See "Incredible Creatures that Defy Evolution"

2. Jesus Christ of Nazareth

Let us look at Jesus. It is a historical fact that Jesus of Nazareth existed, preached, and was executed by the Romans at the insistence of the Jewish leaders. Secular history says this much.

All Jesus would have had to do to avoid being executed in the most torturous way humans have ever come up with was to say He was not God. That is all. Yet He went to the cross with the words "I am (God)" on His lips.

"Again the high priest asked him, and said unto him, "Art thou the Christ, the Son of the Blessed?" And Jesus said, "I am: and ye shall see the Son of man sitting on the right hand of power, and coming in the clouds of heaven." Mark 14:61

Why would He do this? There are only two possibilities. He either was God or He was not. There is no in between. I am either God or I am not (I will tell you right now that I am not). You are either God or you are not. The chair I am sitting in is either God or it is not. There is no in between.

If Jesus was not God, He either knew He was not or He did not know He was not. Again, there is no in-between. He was either a liar, a lunatic or He really was Lord.

Liars, con-artists, are capable of convincing large numbers of people that they are divine. But they all have one thing in common: a strong sense of Self Preservation. A liar of the magnitude Christ would have had to be to pull off the things He did, would have been able to work out a deal with the Jews to avoid being crucified. The fact that He didn't even try shows that the man actually believed what He was saying. Anyone

2. Jesus Christ of Nazareth

who honestly believes He is God (enough to go to the Cross for that belief) is either coo-coo or God Himself. No alternatives.

The level of insanity that convinces a man He is God (strongly enough to override the self preservation instinct) is called Complex, Paranoid Schizophrenia. We have many examples of this disease available for study. Charles Manson is probably the most famous modern case. I once saw a filmed interview of the man. No doubt about it. He is NUTS. He couldn't carry one thought to completion. He changed subjects in the middle of every sentence. All victims of Complex, Paranoid Schizophrenia have one thing in common; they are very violent. Charles Manson committed his crimes (slaughtering a houseful of people) trying to start a race war that would allow him to take over the world.

He who lives by the sword shall die by the sword.
Love your neighbor as yourself.
Do good to them that wrongfully use you.
Turn the other cheek.

I could go on and on with quotes from Christ. Do these sound like the rantings of a violent lunatic? What about the results of His teaching? **"You shall know a tree by the fruit it bears."** Christianity has been the greatest force for peace and brotherly love all over the world[2]. Christianity is responsible for the elimination of cannibalism. It has stopped countless feuds and wars[3].

---

[2] Please see the next chapter.
[3] Please see http://www.voddiebaucham.org/vbm/Blog/Entries/2010/11/6_A_Lesson_in_Historiography__Part_One.html for an excellent refutation of the idea of Christianity causing war, including the Crusades.

2. Jesus Christ of Nazareth

It stopped human sacrifice. Is this the fruit of Complex, Paranoid Schizophrenia? I don't think so.

"Once you have eliminated all the possibilities, what ever remains, no matter how implausible, must be the truth."(Sherlock Holmes)

If Christ was not a liar; if He was not a lunatic; He must be Lord.

"There is a God, and you are not Him."
Rev. Andrew Tracy

The Romans who crucified Christ were experts at execution. Those soldiers would have lost their heads if they did not do it right, so they always made sure they did. Christ was dead when He was removed from the cross.

They placed Him in a tomb and rolled a stone so heavy that three healthy women (who were used to the normal hard labor of the pre-electronic age) were concerned they would not be able to move it away enough to get in. They sealed the tomb with wax and placed guards around it that, again, would loose their heads if they did not do their job right. Christ was not in a coma, as some have claimed. There is no way He could have moved that boulder to get out, even if He had been perfectly healthy, and especially not just three days after the ordeal of the cross (with no water, food or medicine in the mean time).

The disciples did not steal the body. The soldiers (somewhere between 12 and 20 of them) would have killed them if they had tried (and these are the same men who had just run away when Jesus was arrested.

2. Jesus Christ of Nazareth

Hardly the examples of courage necessary to attack trained soldiers.)

Every disciple but John[4] was executed for claiming Christ was alive. Again, these men's teachings were those of sane men ("Love your neighbor as yourself"), yet they died for the belief that Christ rose from the dead. They obviously believed it. In addition, they had just spent three and a half years living day and night with Christ. They could not have been fooled about His identity[5]. When they said they saw their Lord AFTER His crucifixion, all reasonable evidence says that is exactly what they saw.

---

[4] There is a story of John being boiled in oil and living. This a miraculous event and a cool story. However, I can find no reliable verification that the event actually happened.

[5] See "Evidence that Demands a Verdict" by Josh McDowell. A very good and highly recommended book for both those just beginning their walk with God and those who are more experienced.

3. The Truth Of Christian Wars And Violence

There have been many accusations of Christianity causing many, many wars throughout history. I have even heard It accused of being the biggest cause of violence throughout history. Let's examine that belief.

Stalin was an Atheist and was responsible for the deaths of 23 million people.

Mao Zedong was an Atheist and responsible for the deaths of 40-70 million people.

Castro is an Atheist and responsible for 2000-97,000 deaths.

Pol Pot was an Atheist and responsible for 1,700,000 deaths.

Kim Il Sung is an Atheist and responsible for 1,600,000 deaths.

Atheism views humans as nothing more than animals, resources for the state to use as it sees fit. This has resulted in the above tragedies just in the last century. I think before anyone tries to call the Christian culture "the biggest cause of war and death" they had better deal with these facts of just the twentieth century.

If a man declares himself a Jew yet refuses to be circumcised, eats pork, and works on the Sabbath, is he a Jew? Well, he might be a biological descendent of Abraham, but no one would call his religion "Judaism." The Holy books of the Jews outline what a religious Jew is and anyone who does not follow those laws is not a Religious Jew, no matter what his ancestry or his claims.

3. Christian War

If a man declares himself a Muslim yet never prays (much less the required five times per day), doesn't follow any of the dietary laws or fast at Ramadan, is he a Muslim? Again, the foundational documents of the faith have defined what a Muslim is and no matter what a person says, if they do not follow those rules, they are not a member of that faith.

What is the definition of "Christian"? The Holy Book of all Christians, The Bible, tells us. Specifically, our founder Himself tells us:

"By this shall all men know that ye are my disciples, if ye have love one to another." (John 13:35), and

"...Thou shalt love the Lord thy God with all thy heart, and with all thy soul, and with all thy strength, and with all thy mind; and thy neighbor as thyself." (Luke 10:27),

"Ye shall know them by their fruits. Do men gather grapes of thorns, or figs of thistles?" (Matthew 7:16), and the Apostle Paul tells us

"The fruit of the Spirit is love, joy, peace, longsuffering, gentleness, goodness, faith, meekness, temperance: against such there is no law. And they that are Christ's have crucified the flesh with the affections and lusts." (Galatians 5:22-24)

Noah Webster's Original 1828 Dictionary defines "Christian" as:

1) A believer in the religion of Christ.

2) A professor of his belief in the religion of Christ.

3) A real disciple of Christ; one who believes in the truth of the Christian religion, and studies to follow

the example, and obey the precepts, of Christ; a believer in Christ who is characterized by real piety.

4) In a general sense, the word Christians includes all who are born in a Christian country or of Christian parents.

(This last one is not speaking of religious Christians, but cultural Christians. They are NOT members of the Faith of Christ.)

And the Strong's concordance tells us the linguistic definition of the word (from the original Greek) is:

1) Christian, a follower of Christ

So, according to the Christian Holy Book and by official definition a person can not honestly claim to be a Christian unless he 1) Loves God more than anything else and 2) Loves his neighbor as much as himself.

Is it possible for someone to claim to be a Christian and not be? Of course.

"Every tree that bringeth not forth good fruit is hewn down, and cast into the fire.

"Wherefore by their fruits ye shall know them.

"Not every one that saith unto me, 'Lord, Lord,' shall enter into the kingdom of heaven; but he that doeth the will of my Father which is in heaven.

"Many will say to me in that day, 'Lord, Lord, have we not prophesied in thy name? And in thy name have cast out devils? And in thy name done many wonderful works?'

"And then will I profess unto them, I never knew you: depart from me, ye that work iniquity."
Matthew 7:19-23

3. Christian War

I could claim to be a truck but that doesn't give me four wheels and a bed. I could go to the local McDonalds but that doesn't make me a Big Mac. In order for my claim to be a Christian to be true, I MUST:
- 1) Love God more than anything else.
- 2) Love my neighbor as much as myself.
- 3) Show increasing love, joy, peace, patience, gentleness, goodness, faith, meekness and self-control in my life.

So let's look at some of the accusations of violent Christians and "Christian wars."

Hitler. A common claim is that Hitler was a Christian. It is true that he said he was during his election campaign. However, the man never once exhibited any of the above requirements of a religious Christian and it is well known that he engaged in occultic activities (otherwise known as Satan worship.) Certainly killing millions of people (including around one million for standing on the above Christian principles) disqualifies him from being classified as a Christian. The fact is that the man's true "religion" was political power. He did whatever was necessary to get and keep control. That is what he worshipped, not any God of any definition. If that meant he had to claim to be Christian, Buddhist, Atheist, or a Martian, he would have done it.

The Crusades. Whenever reading about the Crusades keep in mind the difference between a "Cultural Christian" (Webster's fourth definition) and a true follower of Christ (Webster's first three definitions). The Ottoman Empire attacked and sacked Jerusalem, enslaving the non-Muslim inhabitants. There was a call for help sent to Europe. The POLITICAL powers of

3. Christian War

state (The Pope, king of France, King of England, etc) responded with armies to rescue these people. Yes, atrocities were committed by people who claimed to be Christian. But war is atrocious by nature. There is simply no way to conduct a war without blood shed. Both sides were quite violent.

Many political gains were attempted by both sides also. In fact, most of the crusades would have happened just the same if we had called the fighting side the "Dodgers and the Yankees" instead of the "Christians and the Muslims." It was all about politics and power, the most evil religion of the world.

Were the soldiers true Christians? I am sure some were. But most were just normal men out to do what was best for themselves and have a little "fun" while doing it. You simply can't chop your neighbor's head off (except for cases of self-defense and even that is iffy and protecting the innocent) and still claim to be a true Christian.

One note, the leaders of the Ottoman Empire were concerned about those in territories captured by the Crusaders. They were treated so well by their captures that the leaders of the Ottoman's were afraid they would convert to Christianity! Even when used politically instead of as God intended, the Name of Christ has influenced people for good.

The Inquisition. Again, Political in totality. In fact, there never was a single "Inquisition." It was a series of events spread out over a number of years. All of the events had a great deal more to do with the fact that Protestant rulers felt no obligation to obey and pay taxes to the Pope. The Pope didn't want a pay cut, so he ordered his followers to recapture the lost territories.

3. Christian War

In fact, some of the conflicts during this time were between two different protestant groups or two different Catholic countries. If a Catholic is fighting a Catholic, it's obviously not a religious war, but highly political.

Martyrs. It is true that individuals have been executed for their faith in Christ by people who claim the Christian title for political reasons. First of all, you can't blame Christianity for the actions of the religiously political. That is blaming the victim for the actions of the aggressor.

You will find, if you take the time to do the research, that every case of "Christian" war and violence would have happened just the same no matter what label the country leaders chose to carry, whether Christian, Muslim, Buddhist or Purple-People-Eater. To apply the same logic that accuses Christians of the violence of the Middle Ages and Reformation to a more modern example, when Sadam Hessian invaded Kuwait it was obviously a religious war. After all, He was a Muslim wasn't he? Well, of course the truth is that he called himself a Muslim but didn't really practice that religion and he invaded Kuwait solely because he wanted a warm water port. It had nothing to do with religion at all. Neither did the wars of the Middle Ages.

It is simply not fair or honest to blame wars caused by the religion of politics on a different religion no matter what label the leaders try to put on themselves.

Have you ever visited the Buddhist hospital in your community? How about the Islamic one? Hindu? You haven't? That's because odds are there aren't any. Now Christian hospitals are a different story. In my

3. Christian War

community the hospitals are split about 50/50 Christian and government. Only the Christian Faith cares enough about others to bother opening hospitals. In fact, check out all the charitable organizations you can find. You will see that the majority were founded by Christians and most are still run by Christians and their principals.

If you ran out of food in your house and had no money there are two places you could go for help; the government and the Christian churches in your community. The other religions are not very likely to help you at all. The only way the atheists help is by raising your taxes for more government programs.

All countries where cannibalism was practiced that have been visited by missionaries for any length of time have seen cannibalism disappear. In fact, Matthew Parris, an avowed Atheist says, "I used to avoid this truth by applauding - as you can - the practical work of mission churches in Africa. It's a pity, I would say, that salvation is part of the package, but Christians black and white, working in Africa, do heal the sick, do teach people to read and write; and only the severest kind of secularist could see a mission hospital or school and say the world would be better without it. I would allow that if faith was needed to motivate missionaries to help, then, fine: but what counted was the help, not the faith.

But this doesn't fit the facts. Faith does more than support the missionary; it is also transferred to his flock. This is the effect that matters so immensely, and which I cannot help observing."[6] He then goes on to say what

---

[6] Please read the whole article at
http://www.timesonline.co.uk/tol/comment/columnists/matthew_parris/article5400568.ece Mr. Parris was raised in Africa and had the experience of seeing

3. Christian War

Africa really needs is not more handouts from wealthy nations but more missionaries. And remember, he's an Atheist!

Christianity brings hope and love to all people where such things do not exist. This has been the eyewitness record since the time of Christ.

The Romans preformed post-natal abortions; they threw unwanted babies off of bridges to drown in the rivers beneath. Christians would wait under the bridges in boats and rescue the babies taking them home to raise as their own.

Whenever the plague hit Europe, it was the Christians (not the "religious" but those in whom neighbors had observed true Christian conversion) who would risk their own lives to nurse the sick and dieing.

It is Christians who have opened orphanages, rescued slaves around the world, nursed the sick, opened schools and preached hope.

No other religion can make any of these claims.

I will concede that Christianity is a bloody religion, though. We are based on the knowledge that we all deserve to die a torturous death and spend eternity in hell. Our Savior, Jesus Christ, chose to die that very bloody death for us. He loved us that much. In this way, and only this way, we do have a bloody religion.

---

the difference missionaries make, eve though it severely violates his religion to acknowledge it.

4. Good and Evil

Did you know there is no such thing as cold? There is only a lack of heat. Did you know there is no such thing as darkness? Only a lack of light. These are scientific facts.

Did you know there is no such thing as evil? Only a lack of God. The devil is completely lacking in any part of God at all. Humans are created in God's image. We have some shadows of the likeness of God. When you choose God, you choose good. When you choose not-God you choose evil. There is no neutral. Only God and evil. Every human, no matter what their upbringing, no matter who their parents, must make that choice for themselves.

Much of the bad that happens is the result of people choosing to deny God. God wanted to be loved. Love requires the choice to not love. If He had not given us the ability to sin, to choose selfishness and cruelty over Him (love and goodness), we would have been no more than chimpanzees or robots. We had to have a choice for it to be true love.

We all choose to deny God at some time or another. This has negative consequences on all those around us. It also separates us from God, as evil is a lack of God. We choose to turn our backs on Him.

In eternity we will all receive just what we have asked for in this life. Those that choose to have a lack of God in their lives will be totally removed from all aspects of God. They will exist in pure evil. Hell.

Those that choose to have God in their lives will have total God in eternity. Pure presence of God. Paradise.[7]

4. Good and Evil

In the 1800's, doctors would go straight from performing an autopsy to delivering babies without washing their hands. It was common for half of the women in a delivery ward to die from post-natal infection. If these doctors had followed God's command to Israel in the Mosaic Law by washing and staying separate for a time after touching the dead, hundreds of women wouldn't have died. Notice, the women did nothing wrong. They did not disobey. Yet they died. When we choose to not listen to God, often others suffer.

There will come a day when all the wrongs will be righted and everything will be squared up. There IS eternal justice. ALL wrongs will be paid for. Yes, those sins that I have committed WILL be paid for. They are horrible sins deserving of the greatest, most awful punishment. But you know what? My sins have already been paid for. You know the story. "He paid the debt He did not owe; I owed a debt I could not pay."

---

[7] From a sermon by Rev. Andy Tracy

5. The Bible

The Bible is the most important document ever written. It is the inspired word of God. God dictated it to righteous men:

"For the prophecy came not in old time by the will of man: but holy men of God spake as they were moved by the Holy Ghost." 2 Peter 1:21

"All scripture is given by inspiration of God, and is profitable for doctrine, for reproof, for correction, for instruction in righteousness." 2 Timothy 3:16

Without the Bible we cannot know God. It tells us of His character and His will in the world and in our lives.

It is also the foundation for our Western Society, American government, and our culture.

It is the greatest piece of literature ever written containing some of the most beautiful prose and poetry ever written (Psalms as well as many individual passages rhyme in Hebrew).

It is essential that we study our Bible regularly. We cannot become too familiar with it. This is how we draw closer to God.

6. Facts About The Bible

The Bible is made up of 66 books: 39 from the Old Testament and 27 from the New.

The Old Testament has thirty-nine books (Memory help: there are three letters in the word old and nine in the word testament= 39).

The first five are called the Pentateuch, and most attribute them to Moses. They are:
- Genesis (Creation through the life of Joseph)
- Exodus (The Israelites leaving Egypt and traveling to the promised land)
- Leviticus (Various laws given by God)
- Numbers (The numbering of Israel and various laws)
- Deuteronomy (Various Laws)

The next twelve are the books of history. They are:
- Joshua (written by Joshua telling of Israel's conquering of the promised land)
- Judges (The history of Israel under the rule of judges, from Joshua to Samuel)
- Ruth (A romance story)
- 1 Samuel (The birth of Samuel, crowning of Saul as the first king)
- 2 Samuel (The story of David and Saul)
- 1Kings (The history of Judah and Israel, from a kingly perspective, from Solomon to the captivity)
- 2 Kings (The history of Judah and Israel, from a kingly perspective, from Solomon to the captivity)
- 1 Chronicles (The history of Judah and Israel, from a priestly perspective, from Solomon to the captivity)
- 2 Chronicles (The history of Judah and Israel, from a priestly perspective, from Solomon to the captivity)

- Ezra (Israel returns to Jerusalem after the Babylonian Captivity.)
- Nehemiah (Israel returns to Jerusalem after the Babylonian Captivity.)
- Ester (A story of God's provision and protection, though the book does not use the name of God anywhere at all.)

Then come the books of poetry:
- Job (The trials of a righteous man and a debate about the nature of God.)
- Psalms (Songs)
- Proverbs (Wise sayings)
- Ecclesiastics (The purpose of life)
- Song of Songs (or Solomon; a love story)

The Major Prophets (each written by the man the book is named after):
- Isaiah (Tells of the coming destruction of many countries as well as the ending history of Judah.)
- Jeremiah (Tells of the coming destruction of Judah and of its actual end.)
- Lamentations (written by Jeremiah to mourn the death of the king.)
- Ezekiel (many prophecies from the end of Judah to the coming of Christ.)
- Daniel (the story of the Captivity and prophecies concerning the rest of the history of the Israelite people).

And the Minor Prophets (each written by the man the book is named after):
- Hosea (Prophecy of the coming Assyrian Captivity and an example of God's love for Israel.)

6. Facts About the Bible

- Joel (A description of a coming plague, a call to repentance, and prophecy of the coming Messiah.)
- Amos (The shepherd prophet; coming judgment on Israel's enemies and Israel herself. A call to repentance.)
- Obadiah (Judgment pronounced on Edom.)
- Jonah (A story about rebellion and redemption.)
- Micah (The story of Israel's sin, judgment and restoration.)
- Nahum (Nineveh is doomed.)
- Habakkuk (Prophecy of Judah's destruction.)
- Zephaniah (Prophecy of Israel's destruction and restoration.)
- Haggai (An exhortation for the restored Israel to finish the Temple.)
- Zechariah (Prophecy of the coming Messiah and His work.)
- Malachi (God's answers to man's questions. A call to righteousness.)

The New Testament has twenty-seven books (Memory help: three letters in the word new times nine letters in the word testament equals twenty-seven.)

The first four books are about the life of Christ, are named after the authors and are called the Gospels:
- Matthew (From the Hebrew perspective.)
- Mark (From the Roman perspective.)
- Luke (From the Greek perspective.)
- John (From the Savior's perspective.)

The one book of History:
- Acts (The history of the early church. Could be called the second half of the book of Luke.)

6. Facts About the Bible

The Pauline (written by Paul) epistles (letters):
- Romans (Written to the church at Rome. The "Constitution of the Christian Church.")
- 1 Corinthians (Written to the church at Corinth. Practical Theology.)
- 2 Corinthians (Information and Instruction to the Corinthian Church.)
- Galatians (Written to the church at Galatia. Justification is by Grace, not Law.)
- Ephesians (Written to the church at Ephesus. Explanation of relationships and roles.)
- Philippians (Written to the church at Philippi. Joy in the Christian walk.)
- Colossians (Written to the church at Colossae. Salvation is through Christ alone.)
- 1 Thessalonians (Written to the church at Thessalonica. Correct doctrine and instruction to the church.)
- 2 Thessalonians (Written to the church at Thessalonica. More of the same.)
- 1 Timothy (Written to his apprentice Timothy. The Leadership manual for the Church.)
- 2 Timothy (Written to his apprentice Timothy. Paul's final words and instructions to Timothy.)
- Titus (Written to his friend Titus. Much the same theme as in Timothy.)
- Philemon (Written to his friend Philemon about a runaway slave who had come to Christ.)

- Hebrews (We don't know for sure who wrote this book. Some attribute it to Paul. Others to Apollos, Timothy, or other ministers of the time. It was written to Hebrews still in Jerusalem.)

6. Facts About the Bible

The non-Pauline epistles (named after the authors):
- James (Practical application of the Gospel.)
- 1 Peter (To persecuted Christians.)
- 2 Peter (An exhortation to continue growing in God.)
- 1 John (Strengthening believers and refuting heretics.)
- 2 John ("Stay the course.")
- 3 John (Commendation to Gaius and Condemnation to Diotrephes.)
- Jude (Encouragement to remain doctrinally pure.)

One book of Prophecy (Written by Jesus' disciple John):
- Revelation (Foretelling the destruction of Jerusalem and the ending of the Jewish nation.)

7. Fun Facts

The longest book of the Bible is Psalms-150 chapters.

The shortest book of the Bible is 2 John with one chapter, 13 verses.

The longest chapter of the Bible is Psalms 119 with 150 verses.

The shortest chapter of the Bible is Psalms 117 with 2 verses. This is also the middle chapter of the Bible.

The middle verse of the Bible is Psalms 118:8.

The shortest verse in the Bible is John 11:35- "Jesus wept."

The longest verse is Ester 8:9 containing 90 words.

The Bible Contains:
⇒ 3,566,480 letters
⇒ 773,693 words
⇒ 31,102 verses
⇒ 1,189 chapters: 250 in the new, and 939 in the old

The word "and" appears 46,277 times.

Reverend appears once.

"Lord" appears 1,855 times.

The longest word is: Mahershalalhashbaz. It is found in Isaiah 8:1 and has 18 letters (It is a name).

The 21 verse of Ezra 7 contains all the letters of the alphabet except J.

Ester has no mention God.

Verses 8, 15, 21, and 31 Psalms 107 are alike.

Every verse in Psalms 136 ends the same.

The 19th chapter of 2 Kings and Isaiah 37 are almost identical.

7. Fun Facts

There are about 200 direct quotes in the New Testament from the Old Testament.

The first Bible printed is this country was in 1663 in an Indian language.

8. Where Did Our Bible Come From?

God dictated the Bible to men from ancient times to the first century A.D. There is some disagreement on whether the first part written down is the Ten Commandments (written by God's own hand and given to Moses; the most popular view) or if Adam and his descendents actually wrote the parts of Genesis concerning their own lives and Moses later compiled them into one book. Either way, God then dictated the next four books to Moses. These first five books are called the Pentateuch (literally- "five books."). Job is believed by many to be a contemporary of these books.

The rest of the Old Testament was finished and pretty much in the form we know it today (though in ancient Hebrew, not English) by 400 B.C. Scribes painstakingly copied the originals checking letter for letter, destroying entire panels if they got even two letters too close together. This attention to detail was carried into the Greek Septuagint. We know the most ancient copies, then, are accurate.

For even more verification, the Dead Sea scrolls were discovered in the mid 1900's. These are documents written between 150BC and 70AD including many of the books of the Old Testament. Some of these have been translated into modern languages with the discovery that our current Bible matches exactly.

The New Testament was completed (in Greek) by the end of the first century A.D. The churches and their leaders agreed that certain letters and documents were valuable to all the churches and made exact copies to share with each other. These were assembled into the New Testament.

The most ancient copies of the complete Bible we have today are the Codex Alexandrius and the Codex

8. Where Did Our Bible Come From?

Sinaiticus in the British Museum Library in London, and the Codex Vaticanus in the Vatican. They date back to approximately the 300's AD.

In 382 AD, Saint Jerome, translated the New Testament from its original Greek into Latin. This translation became known as the "Latin Vulgate." This is about the time the Catholic Church was founded. At this time they added what Protestants call the Apocrypha, extra books not excepted as scripture by anyone but the Catholic church.

By 500 AD the Bible had been translated into over 500 languages. By 600 AD, it was only available in the Latin Vulgate. The Catholic Church refused to allow the scripture to be available in any other language. Those in possession of non-Latin scriptures were executed (generally by torture and burning).

9. The English Bible

The first English language Bible manuscripts were hand-written in the 1380's AD by John Wycliffe. With the help of his followers (called the Lollards) Wycliffe produced dozens of English language manuscript copies of the scriptures.

When John Hus (one of Wycliffe's followers) was burned at the stake in 1415, they used Wycliffe's manuscript Bibles as kindling for the fire. The last words of John Hus were, "In 100 years, God will raise up a man whose calls for reform cannot be suppressed." Almost exactly 100 years later, in 1517, Martin Luther nailed his famous 95 "Theses of Contention" (a list of 95 issues of heretical theology and crimes of the Roman Catholic Church) onto the church door at Wittenberg, Germany. The prophecy of Hus had come true!

Martin Luther was the first man to print the Bible in the German language. In that same year seven people were burned at the stake by the Roman Catholic Church (political government) for the crime of teaching their children to say the Lord's Prayer in English rather than Latin.[8]

The first book off of Johannes Gutenberg's printing press was a Latin Vulgate Bible. Gutenberg's Bibles were very beautiful, since each leaf Gutenberg printed was later colorfully hand-illustrated.

The scholar Erasmus wanted to correct the corrupt Latin Vulgate. He assembled the New Testament in Greek from several partial manuscripts. In 1516 he published a Greek-Latin Parallel New Testament where the Latin part was his own rendering

---
[8] Foxe's Book of Martyrs

9. The English Bible

of the text, not the Vulgate. This Greek-Latin New Testament focused attention on just how corrupt and inaccurate the Latin Vulgate had become, and how important it was to go back and use the original Greek (New Testament) and Hebrew (Old Testament) languages to maintain accuracy. It also showed how important it was to have the Bible in the language of the common people no matter what that language is.

William Tyndale was the spiritual leader of the Army of Reformers. He was a true scholar and a genius, so fluent in eight languages that he could pass as a native in any of them. He is frequently referred to as the "Architect of the English Language", (even more so than Shakespeare) as so many of the phrases Tyndale coined are still in our language today.

Tyndale wanted to use the 1516 Erasmus non-Vulgate text as a source to translate and print the New Testament in English. He was forced to flee England because of this work. Tyndale showed up on Luther's doorstep in Germany in 1525, and by year's end had translated the New Testament into English. The 1525 Tyndale New Testament became the first printed edition of the scripture in the English language.

These Bibles were burned as soon as the authorities could confiscate them, but copies trickled through anyway. One actually ended up in the bedroom of King Henry VIII.

The more the King and the Anglican Church (Henry VIII's replacement for Catholicism) resisted its distribution, the more curious the public at large became. The church declared it contained thousands of errors and they torched as many as they could get their hands on. In fact, they burned them because they could find no errors at all and showed that their tyrannical rule

9. The English Bible

was wrong. The penalty for even owning a Tyndale Bible was death by burning.

Today, there are only two known copies left of Tyndale's 1525-26 First Edition.

How did Tyndale fund his printing? The king's men bought all the Bibles they could to burn, leaving a profit to print even more with! Books and Bibles flowed into England in bales of cotton and sacks of flour.

Eventually, Tyndale was caught and burned at the stake in 1536. His last words were, "Oh Lord, open the King of England's eyes". This prayer would be answered just three years later.

Myles Coverdale and John "Thomas Matthew" Rogers had been loyal followers of Tyndale. They continued his project. Coverdale finished translating the Old Testament, and in 1535 he printed the first complete Bible in the English language. This first complete English Bible (printed on October 4, 1535) is known as the Coverdale Bible.

John Rogers translated the Bible into English directly from Hebrew and Greek. He printed it under the same pseudonym Tyndale had once used, "Thomas Matthew." This was appropriate since it is a composite made up of Tyndale's Pentateuch and New Testament (1534-1535 edition) and Coverdale's Bible and some of Roger's own translation of the text. It is known as the Matthew-Tyndale Bible.

The Church and king gave up. In 1539, Thomas Cranmer, the Archbishop of Canterbury, hired Myles Coverdale at the bequest of King Henry VIII to publish the "Great Bible". It became the first English Bible authorized for public use. It was chained to the pulpit in every church and a reader was even provided so that the illiterate could hear the Word of God in plain

9. The English Bible

English. Cranmer's Bible, published by Coverdale, was known as the Great Bible due to its great size. It was over 14 inches tall. Seven editions of this version were printed between April of 1539 and December of 1541.

10. The Bible Comes of Age

In the 1550's, many reformers took refuge in Geneva, Switzerland. This is where John Foxe wrote and published his "Foxe's Book of Martyrs," which is to this day the only exhaustive reference work on the persecution and martyrdom of Early Christians and Protestants from the first century up to the mid-16th century. With the protection of John Calvin and John Knox, Foxe, Coverdale, Thomas Sampson and William Whittingham and others determined to produce a Bible that would educate their families while they continued in exile.

The New Testament was completed in 1557, and the complete Geneva Bible was first published in 1560. This was the first Bible to add numbered verses to the chapters, so that referencing specific passages would be easier. Every chapter was also accompanied by extensive marginal notes and references so thorough and complete that the Geneva Bible is also considered the first English "Study Bible". William Shakespeare quotes from it hundreds of times in his plays. The Geneva Bible became the Bible of choice for over 100 years of English speaking Christians. It retains over 90% of William Tyndale's original English translation. The Geneva holds the honor of being the first Bible taken to America, and the Bible of the Puritans and Pilgrims. It is truly the "Bible of the Protestant Reformation."

With the end of Queen Mary's bloody reign, the reformers could safely return to England. The Anglican Church, now under Queen Elizabeth I, tolerated the printing and distribution of Geneva version Bibles in England. The marginal notes, which were vehemently against the institutional Church of the day, did not rest

10. The Bible Comes of Age

well with the rulers of the day however. A Bible with a less inflammatory tone was desired, and since the copies of the Great Bible were getting to be decades old, a new version was ordered. In 1568, a revision of the Great Bible known as the Bishop's Bible was introduced. This Bible is referred to as the "rough draft of the King James Version."

By the 1580's, the Catholic Church saw that it had lost the battle and the Bible would be available in the English language. In 1582, the Church of Rome decided that if the Bible was to be available in English, they would at least have an official Roman Catholic English translation. And so, using the corrupt and inaccurate Latin Vulgate as the only source text, they went on to publish an English Bible with all the distortions and corruptions that Erasmus had revealed and warned of 75 years earlier. Because it was translated at the Roman Catholic College in the city of Rheims, it was known as the Rheims New Testament. The Douay Old Testament was translated by the Church of Rome in 1609 at the College in the city of Douay. The combined product is commonly referred to as the "Doway/Rheims" Version. In 1589, Dr. William Fulke of Cambridge published the "Fulke's Refutation", in which he printed in parallel columns the Bishops Version along side the Rheims Version, attempting to show the error and distortion of the Roman Church's corrupt compromise of an English version of the Bible.

11. The King James

When Queen Elizabeth I died, Prince James VI of Scotland became King James I of England. The Protestant clergy requested a new translation to replace the Bishop's Bible. They knew that the Geneva Version had won the hearts of the people because of its excellent scholarship, accuracy, and exhaustive commentary, but they did not want the controversial marginal notes (proclaiming the Pope as Anti-Christ, etc.) Essentially, the leaders of the church desired a Bible for the people, with scriptural references only for word clarification or cross-references.

This "translation to end all translations" was the result of the combined effort of about fifty scholars. They took into consideration: The Tyndale New Testament, The Coverdale Bible, The Matthews Bible, The Great Bible, The Geneva Bible, and even the Rheims New Testament. From 1605 to 1606 the scholars engaged in private research. From 1607 to 1609 the work was assembled. In 1610 the work went to press, and in 1611 the first of the huge (16 inch tall) pulpit Bibles, known today as "The 1611 King James Bible," came off the printing press. Starting just one year later, printing began on the earliest normal-sized King James Bibles. These were produced so individuals could have their own personal copy of the Bible.

The King James ended up being 95% the same as the Geneva (which was 90% Tyndales) with influence by the Roman Catholic Rheims New Testament. Nevertheless, the King James Bible became the most printed book in the history of the world, and the only book with one billion copies in print.

11. The King James

In fact, for over 250 years the King James Version reigned without much of a rival.

One little-known fact, is that for the past 200 years, all King James Bibles published in America are actually the 1769 Baskerville spelling and wording revision of the 1611. The publishers add the original "1611" preface without any mention of this revision so as to not hurt sales. Most Americans would simply not be able to read the 1611 version due to the different spellings.

The first Bible printed in America was done in the native Algonquin Indian Language by John Eliot in 1663. The first English language Bible to be printed in America by Robert Aitken in 1782 was a King James Version.

12. Our Modern Versions

After finishing his "Dictionary of the English Language," Noah Webster set about to make his own translation of the Bible. Unfortunately, people were just too used to the KJV to accept it.

England planned a replacement for their King James Bible in the 1880's, the English Revised Version (E.R.V.). This would be the first English language Bible to be accepted as a post-King James Version, modern-English Bible.

The Americans responded to England's E.R.V. Bible by publishing the nearly-identical American Standard Version (A.S.V.) in 1901. It was widely-accepted and embraced by churches throughout America. In 1971, it was again revised and called New American Standard Version Bible (often referred to as the N.A.S.V. or N.A.S.B. or N.A.S.). This Bible is considered by many evangelical Christian scholars and translators, to be the most accurate, word-for-word translation of the original Greek and Hebrew scriptures into the modern English language. It remains the most popular version among theologians, professors, scholars, and seminary students today. Some, however, think it is too hard to read.

To fix that problem, the New International Version (N.I.V.) was produced in 1973, which was offered as a "dynamic equivalent" translation into modern English. The N.I.V. was designed not for "word-for-word" accuracy, but rather, for "phrase-for-phrase" accuracy, and ease of reading even at a Junior High-School reading level. It was meant to appeal to a broader, less-educated cross-section of the general public. Critics of the N.I.V. often jokingly refer to it as the "Nearly

12. Our Modern Versions

Inspired Version", but that has not stopped it from becoming the most popular, non-KJV Bible.

To translate the NIV, the Masoretic, Septuagint, Aquila, Symmachus, Theodotion, the Vulgate, the Syriac Peshitta, Targums, and (for the Psalms) the *Juxta Hebraica* of Jerome were consulted. The non-Masoretic texts were followed where they were more likely to be correct.

In 1982, Thomas Nelson Publishers tried to produce a KJV with the archaic pronouns changed to modern versions and obscure words updated. However, copywrite laws required that they change more than that. The result is called the "New King James Version".

In 2002, a major attempt was made to bridge the gap between the simple readability of the N.I.V., and the extremely precise accuracy of the N.A.S.B. This translation is called the English Standard Version (E.S.V.) and is rapidly gaining popularity for its readability and accuracy.

There have been many "paraphrase Bibles;" Bibles that attempt to put the Word into modern English to make it more understandable. This will most likely continue. Some of these are The Message (my favorite paraphrase Bible), The Simple English Bible, and The Good News for Modern Man. They have their place in introducing people to the Word of God and giving a different perspective on Scripture, but should not be used for more mature work. The deeper, more accurate translations are better for getting to the deeper truths.

13. A Comparison

Here are some comparisons of different English translations of John 3:16:

- **The Message:** "This is how much God loved the world: He gave his Son, his one and only Son. And this is why: so that no one need be destroyed; by believing in him, anyone can have a whole and lasting life."
- **Good News For Modern Man:** "For God loved the World so much that he gave his only Son, so that everyone who believes in him may not die but have eternal life."
- **The Amplified:** "For God so greatly loved and dearly prized the world that He [even] gave up His only begotten ([a]unique) Son, so that whoever believes in (trusts in, clings to, relies on) Him shall not perish (come to destruction, be lost) but have eternal (everlasting) life."
- **The New Living:** "For God loved the world so much that he gave his one and only Son, so that everyone who believes in him will not perish but have eternal life."
- **Young's Literal:** "for God did so love the world, that His Son -- the only begotten -- He gave, that every one who is believing in him may not perish, but may have life age-during."
- **New American Standard:** "For God so loved the world, that He gave His only begotten Son, that whoever believes in Him should not perish, but have eternal life."
- **The New King James:** "For God so loved the world that He gave His only begotten son, that whoever

13. A Comparison

believes in Him should not perish but have everlasting life."

- **The New International Version:** "For God so loved the world that he gave his one and only Son, that whoever believes in him shall not perish but have eternal life."
- **The current "old" King James:** "For God so loved the world that he gave his only begotten son that whosoever believeth in him shall not perish but have everlasting life."
- **1st Ed. King James (1611):** "For God so loued the world, that he gaue his only begotten Sonne: that whosoeuer beleeueth in him, should not perish, but haue euerlasting life."
- **Rheims (1582):** "For so God loued the vvorld, that he gaue his only-begotten sonne: that euery one that beleeueth in him, perish not, but may haue life euerlasting"
- **Geneva (1560):** "For God so loueth the world, that he hath geuen his only begotten Sonne: that none that beleue in him, should peryshe, but haue euerlasting lyfe."
- **Great Bible (1539):** "For God so loued the worlde, that he gaue his only begotten sonne, that whosoeuer beleueth in him, shulde not perisshe, but haue euerlasting lyfe."
- **Tyndale (1534):** "For God so loveth the worlde, that he hath geven his only sonne, that none that beleve in him, shuld perisshe: but shuld have everlastinge lyfe."
- **Wycliff (1380):** "for god loued so the world; that he gaf his oon bigetun sone, that eche man that bileueth in him perisch not: but haue euerlastynge liif,"

13. A Comparison

When it comes right down to it, the most important message, that Jesus died for our sins, comes through loud and clear in any translation. God made sure of that.

14. Which Bible to Use

The King James is the closest to the original of all the most commonly available translations. However, there are no differences between the translations that would make the difference between heaven and hell.

I like the King James Bible. For one, it is the Bible I grew up with and I am familiar with it. Others just sound weird to me.

Secondly, I believe the Word of God deserves to be presented in the most beautiful form the English language has ever taken; Shakespearian English (This was not quite the common dialect of the 1600s by the way. It was the theatrical form of the language.)

Third, its poetic cadence is easier to memorize than our modern translations. You tell me what sticks in the brain better;

"First this: God created the Heavens and Earth-- all you see, all you don't see. Earth was a soup of nothingness, a bottomless emptiness, an inky blackness. God's Spirit brooded like a bird above the watery abyss." (The Message)

or

"In the beginning God created the heavens and the earth. And the earth was without form and void and darkness was upon the face of the deep." (KJV)

Though the meaning is the same, the later has a poetic cadence that makes it easier to memorize.

Fourth, it uses easier words than the modern translations do. Yes, that's right, easier words. For example, in the story of the ordination of King Saul, The NIV tells us he hid among the "luggage." The KJV uses the word "stuff." There are many examples of this throughout the Word. The King James only has about

8000 different words as opposed to the NIV, which has over 14,000 different words.

In comparisons of different translations for grade level placement, one scholar came to the following assessment:

The King James averages grade level 5.8 (fifth grade, eighth month)
New International Version- 8.4
New American Standard Bible- 6.1
The English Version-7.2
New KJV- 6.9

A comparison of words in the KJV and the NASB:

	KJV	NASB
Matt.1:11, 1:17	carried away	deportation
Matt.1:20	Thought	considered
Matt.2:1, 2:7	wise men	Magi
Mark. 2:21	New	unshrunk
Matt. 2:16	Coasts	environs
Luke 3:17, Matt.	Fan	winnowing fork
Luke 11:33, Matt	Bushel	peck-measure
Matt. 5:19	Break	Annuls
Matt. 5:21	kill	Murder
Luke 5:29, Matt.	Sat	recline at the table
Matt. 8:32	go	Be gone
Matt. 9:13, 12:7	mercy	Compassion
Matt. 9:17	Bottles	Wineskins
Matt. 9:18	certain ruler	synagogue official
Mark 5:25, Matt.	issue of blood	Hemorrhage

[source: New Age Bible Versions, G.A.Riplinger, 1993 (690 pgs),[9]

14. Which Bible to Use

There are some problems with the KJV, however. For one, the men who translated it added a few verses in, originally as footnotes, that have since been incorporated into the main text. 1 John 5:7 is one of those. This is due to the influence of the very inaccurate Latin Vulgate.

Secondly, many complain about the "thee's and thou's." I don't have a problem because I am used to them. However, it even helped me to learn that they were not just fancy ways of saying "you."

In the sixteenth-century English the KJV was originally translated into, thee, thou, thine, and thy were singular pronouns while you and yours were plural. This makes many verses, especially those referring to God, much plainer to understand.

---

[9] (This is only a small part of this chart. For the whole thing see http://www.hsnp.com/gok/bible18.html)

15. Biblical Interpretation

Proper interpretation and understanding of the Bible requires three basic tools; understanding of biblical context, understanding of historical context, and understanding of original languages.

In order to understand scripture we must always take the context of scripture into account. What was the author saying in the whole chapter, the whole book? Who was he talking to? Why?

There once was a man who wanted to know God's will in his life. He randomly opened his Bible. It fell to the scripture where Judas killed himself. Wondering what this meant for him, he randomly opened his Bible again. This time it fell open to the scripture "...Then said Jesus unto him, Go, and do thou likewise. ." (Luke 10:37) Was this God telling him to kill himself? Of course not. You must take scripture in its context. You CAN NOT take a verse here and a verse there and put them together to form a doctrine. This is mis-handling of the Word of God.

God tells some people to do things He doesn't want everyone to do. For example, all believers are not to go preach to Nineveh as Jonah was told to do. Nor build a large boat and gather a bunch of animals onto it. Nor lay in the middle of the city, naked, eating nothing but bread and not talking for an entire year like Ezekiel was told to. We must pay attention to whom each scripture was written to and why. The moral lessons taught in every scripture can be applied to our lives, but the fact of the scripture applies to who it was written to. The rule of context is that context rules.

The second rule of biblical interpretation requires that we see what was happening in history. For example, when God told Jonah to go to Nineveh (the

15. Biblical Interpretation

capital of the Assyrian empire), it was because the Ninavites were very cruel conquerors of the entire region. They would cut the heads off of the leaders of each city-state they conquered and often torture the inhabitants. God was fed up. He sent Jonah to warn them to change their ways or else. Of course we know that it worked; they repented and God spared the city. Well, for a while anyway. History tells us that the city was destroyed for its cruelty a generation or so later, after they forgot God and had gone back to their old ways. Jonah didn't even want to give them the chance to repent. He was a bigot and wanted them destroyed immediately. He was not afraid of them as many children's Bibles tell us.

We must understand the history surrounding an event to truly understand what the Bible is telling us (In the case of Jonah, God loves everyone no matter what their nationality and we should obey Him no matter what).

The third tool we need to really understand the Bible is a knowledge of original languages. This is not so hard as it used to be. Any Internet-connected computer has access to a Strong's Concordance (and they are available in book-form from any book seller for as little as $10.00). This is a list of each word in the Bible and its location AND its definition in the original language. You simply look up the words in a verse and see what the original author meant.

16. The Cannon Bible

There are those who claim to believe God and the Bible but who want to change the Word of God.

The most extreme are probably the "Red Letter" people. They claim to only read and follow the red words of the Bible, the exact Words of Jesus.

Another group says they do not read any of the Old Testament, as it doesn't apply to us today.

Yet another group goes the other way and says they follow the whole Bible…except the Pauline epistles as Paul was some sort of evil, ego-maniac (Never mind that the Apostle Peter called Paul's writings "wisdom given unto him." 2 Peter 3:15).

Then there are those who want to add to the Bible. The argument goes, "We find truth outside of the Bible, so, though the Bible is infallible, other things can be used for doctrine also." These especially want to use the books of Enoch, Jassur, and the gospels of Timothy and James.

My first response to the last group is "How do you know that the particular document you are holding is the one it claims to be?" For example, there are four completely different books that claim to be the book of Enoch. How are we supposed to know which one was written by Noah's Great-grandfather? If indeed any of them really were.

God is all-powerful. God is all knowing, from the moment of creation to the end of time. He knew that the set of documents we call the Cannon Bible today were the ones that would be used to spread the knowledge of Him to the planet throughout the last 2000 years of history. I believe He had complete control of what was contained in that Book.

16. The Cannon Bible

The Old Testament was assembled into the form we know it shortly after the time of Alexander the Great. If the "book of Enoch" held truths we could base doctrine on, why didn't He include it in the Septuagint? Why was it left out and only available to us, now, 2500 years later? Why deprive those millions of people or this resource? It seems much more likely to me that there are things contained in Enoch (which ever one is actually the real one) that are not true and that will even lead us into dangerous teachings. This is true, also, of books written after the time of Christ that were not included in the New Testament. The New Testament was complete in the form we know it by AD 100. That is, the churches of the first century gathered together and copied by hand those documents they felt God telling them to share with each other. We know that they left out at least one Pauline epistle (2 Corinthians; what we have is actually 1 and 3 Corinthians.) They likely left out others also. God had those letters that He didn't want included in the Bible lost very close to the time they were written. With the church's determination to hold onto the writings of the apostles, this was a miracle in itself.

Paul says in Timothy that, "All scripture is given by God and is profitable for doctrine, for reproof, for correction, for instruction in righteousness." The extra-cannon books do not meet this stringent requirement.

To the above as well as those who simply find parts of the Bible too uncomfortable to believe (whether the parts that say God commanded the death of entire peoples, or the parts where Paul tells women to obey their hubbies and be keepers at home), God went to all the trouble to preserve those exact documents and you

16. The Cannon Bible

dare to have the gall to say they are worthless? What right do you have to declare, above the authority of all the church leaders for 2000 years, above sincerely intended and highly educated scholars (such as Isaac Newton, Martin Luther, and John Calvin), that some parts of the Bible are wrong? That it contains things it shouldn't? What makes you smarter than them? What gives you this authority? Wouldn't a loving, powerful God have corrected these wrongs long ago instead of waiting 2000 years? Why let so many people continue in fallacy? Why are we "so much smarter?" The fact is we aren't any smarter. We are just more arrogant.

Here is my recommendation: take all your commentaries on the Bible, all your books, and pack them away. Delete all your websites (or at least put them into a folder and don't open them). Then take your Bible out. Read the entire thing cover to cover at least three times. Get your concordance out and look up every unfamiliar word. Get to know the Bible for what it presents itself to be. After that, when you begin to read other resources, be sure you spend more time in the Bible than any other document. Then you won't be susceptible to these false teachings trying to deceive you away from God.

Do you know how they train people to spot counterfeit money? They don't expose them to the counterfeits. They don't study the frauds. They study the real thing. They spend so much time examining real money and are so familiar with the real thing that they spot an imposter immediately.

This is the training you need in the Word of God.

16. The Cannon Bible

"Study to show thyself approved unto God a workman that needeth not be ashamed, rightly dividing the word of truth." 2 Timothy 2:15

"If you continue in my word, then are ye my disciples indeed; and ye shall know the truth, and the truth shall make you free." John 8:32

You find correct facts in many places. You only find truth in the Bible.

17. Bible Helps
The Concordance

A concordance is an assemblage of every word in the Bible in alphabetical order with all of its locations. The Strong's concordance also links you to the original Hebrew or Greek word and gives the definition of that word. This better allows you to know what the author really meant when he wrote that scripture.

Let's say we want to know where the verse "For God so loved the world that He gave His only begotten son, that whosoever believeth in Him shall not perish but shall have ever lasting life." Is found.

First we will pick a word to look up- "world."

In the alphabetical listing we find that the word "world" is listed 249 times. This means that in 249 verses the translators translated a Greek or Hebrew word to mean "world." Forty-six of these are in the Old Testament. In the 203 New Testament occurrences, three different Greek words (represented by three different numbers; 165, 2889, and 3625) were translated into the word "world." By reading the part of each verse listed we find that the one we want is John 3:16. "World" in this verse is number 2889. We turn to the Greek Lexicon in the back and find that this "world" is κόσμος or in the English alphabet; kosmos. It means:

1) An apt and harmonious arrangement or constitution, order, government
2) ornament, decoration, adornment, i.e. the arrangement of the stars, 'the heavenly hosts', as the ornament of the heavens. 1 Peter 3:3
3) The world, the universe
4) The circle of the earth, the earth
5) The inhabitants of the earth, men, the human family

6) The ungodly multitude; the whole mass of men alienated from God, and therefore hostile to the cause of Christ
7) World affairs, the aggregate of things earthly
   a) The whole circle of earthly goods, endowments riches, advantages, pleasures, etc, which although hollow and frail and fleeting, stir desire, seduce from God and are obstacles to the cause of Christ.
8) Any aggregate or general collection of particulars of any sort.
   a) The Gentiles as contrasted to the Jews (Rom. 11:12 etc)
   b) Of believers only, John 1:29; 3:16; 3:17; 6:33; 12:47 1 Cor. 4:9; 2 Cor. 5:19

Strong's comes in several translations.

Thompson Chain Reference Bible

This is the Bible required by many Bible colleges. It is King James.

Down the sides of each page are two columns with numbers and scriptures. The scriptures take you to other scriptures on the same subject as the adjoining verses. The numbers take you to a supplement in the back that lists scriptures by subjects. Before this supplement is a table of contents that lists all the different subjects so you can look up which ever one you need.

The Thompson Chain also has a concordance (not as complete as Strong's), maps, charts about the life of Christ and other prominent Bible characters, summaries of each book in the Bible, and an archeological supplement.

17. Bible Helps
Dickson Bible
In the front is a very good dictionary with scripture references. In the back, the concordance also gives a definition. It has in-verse definitions also. It has "the life of..." outline pages, a chart of tables and measures, a timeline and synopsis of each book and chapter, maps, and other helps. Currently out of print, it can be found on the used book market or there are similar study Bibles available if you know what to look for.

Center reference
These bibles have a column down the middle of the page with small numbers or letters followed by definitions of words in the corresponding scripture and sometimes other verses on the same subjects.

Bible dictionary
This is a dictionary specific to giving you the Biblical definitions of words and terms.

Comparative Bible
This is a Bible that has more than one translation in the same book. It will have one translation in one column and another right next to that. These are good for Bible studies. They have from two to twelve different versions. Occasionaly you can find with two different languages to aid those learning a new tongue (i.e. Spanish/English).

Interlinear Bible
These Bibles contain the Greek or Hebrew text with the direct, word for word English translation immediately below each word.

17. Bible Helps
Bible Atlas

This is a book of maps, pictures and information about the biblical region of the world (modern day Palestine). They usually have different maps of the same area marked for different time periods. For example, one map may be marked for the time of Moses and the next for the time of David.

Chronological Bibles

These are Bibles rearranged so that the scriptures are in the order they were written in. "Canonical" or normal order is roughly chronological until the prophets. A chronological Bible puts the prophets in the middle of Kings and Chronicles where they actually lived and blends Kings and Chronicles into one account instead of two accounts of the same time period. This is more like reading a story or novel and many find it easier to follow what's going on.

Footnotes and Commentaries

These are the opinions of human scholars. They can be very helpful in understanding the scripture, especially the historical context, but you must keep in mind that they are just opinions and not cannon Bible.

18. Dating Creation

We can't know this date for sure, though there are some hints in the Bible and in Creation itself to give us a general number.

If you take all the ages of al the men when their mentioned son was born and add them up you get a time for Creation at roughly 4000BC. This is the youngest the earth could be. However, the odds of each child being born on his father's birthday is slim at best, so we should add partial years into the date. Also, the Bible often calls grandsons the sons of their grandfathers. It is possible these lists of fathers and sons has a few grandson/grandfather relationships. This would also stretch the date. However, you can't stretch it more than a couple of centuries without making the whole list irrelevant. So we could safely say the Bible says the world is around 6000-9000 years old.

Those methods of dating that tell us the earth is much older (on the order of 4 billion years) are all based on very flawed science and assumptions. There is no proof of an old earth. In fact, the decay rate of Carbon 14 should leave us with many fossils with no measurable carbon left in them if the earth is more than 100,000 years old. We have yet to find one sample without measurable Carbon 14. Thus the earth could not possibly be more than 100,000 years old.

The earth should reach Carbon saturation point (the same amount of carbon entering the atmosphere from the sun as leaving it) at 30,000 years of age. We have yet to hit saturation point. Young earth.

Tree ring dates, ice flow dates, lunar dust depths, and several other scientific measures tell us the earth could not possibly be more than a million years old and is closer to 10,000 at most.[10] So we can put the

18. Dating Creation

Creation Account at 4000-8,000 bc. I lean towards no earlier than 5000BC.

---

[10] See the many good books on the subject at the "Creation Research Institute" and "Answers in Genesis" for a more in-depth discussion on the science supporting creation and a young earth.

19. Can We Believe?

There is a God. The human soul demands a God. Even Atheists know in their hearts there is a God. That is why they get so upset at the mention of God. They don't get mad at the mention of Santa Claus, the Easter Bunny, the Tooth fairy, Buddha, Mohammed, or any other religious or fictional character. Only the Christian God angers them. This tells me that in their heart, they know He is true. In fact their very assertion that if there was a God He wouldn't allow evil in the world acknowledges that they know good and evil in their hearts, a sign of the design of God Himself.

Can we believe the Bible? The Bible was written by eyewitnesses to the events they record. This is the gold standard for historical evidence. No other document in the history of the world has been as thoroughly challenged, examined, torn apart, and criticized. Yet it has NEVER been proven wrong. There have been times when people claimed to have proven it wrong. *"King David never existed. He was just a legend"*. Within two years of this statement, archeologists dug up his signet ring; positive, proof he did exist. They have said the same thing about Nineveh, Babylon, and the Hittites. Same results. It almost looks like God is withholding the physical evidence until someone says something in the Bible doesn't exist and then He allows the remains to be discovered to make the scientists look like fools. Who says God doesn't have a sense of humor?

The fact is that, whether they like it or not, science is continually proving more and more of the Bible to be right.

Do you know why so many scientists refuse to believe in God? If they believe in God, they must

19. Can We Believe?

believe there is a right and a wrong. If there is a right and wrong then they must change their lives and their religion. Many scientists who have been challenged to honestly examine the real evidence of science have ended up giving their hearts to God. Others go to extreme lengths to continue to believe in their religion of Atheism. Ever heard the reasons an atheist scientist gives for why *older* fossil layers are often found on top of younger layers? It has to do with multi-thousand ton boulders playing leap frog over thousands of miles without leaving debris trails, skid marks or stress fractures. This is more logical than Noah's flood?!

You know, if we can't believe the Bible, then we can't believe any other ancient document. None of them can stand up to the same standards of examination. If the Bible isn't true, then Buddha, Confucius, Caesar, Hannibal, Justinian, Nero, Plato, Aristotle, Socrates and many, many others never existed. There is no proof of their existence that even comes close to being as scientificly and historically reliable as the Bible.

There are many prophecies in the Bible that have been fullfilled. Only Someone who knew the beginning from the end could have told Isaiah that a man named Cyrus would send the Israelites back to their homeland...seventy years before Cyrus was born!

Jeremiah prophecied that Judah would be in captivity for seventy years, and they were.

Abraham received word that his decendents would be in Egypt 400 years and they were.

Joseph received interpretation of dreams that came true.

Daniel received and recorded several prophecies about the rise and fall of Babylon, Meda-Persia,

19. Can We Believe?

Greece, Syria, and Rome in extreme detail, plus an exact time table for the time of the Messiah. All of this came true exactly as predicted.

The prophecies concerning Christ Himself are mathmaticly impossible for one man to fulfill (He shall come from Nazareth, come up from Egypt, come from Bethlehem for example) and yet Christ fullfilled EVERY ONE!

If the Bible is true historically and scientifically and its prophecies have proven true in the face of astronomical odds, there is no logical reason to doubt it spiritually.

We can believe.

Other Books by Betty's Books:
- **About the Bible** *By Betty Tracy*
- **Auntie's Voice** *By Merriel Haworth*
- **Caring for Your Masterpiece: Nutrition** *By Betty Tracy*
- **Ephesians: Who We Are In Christ** *By Daniel R. Wiltse*
- **First Things First: The Book of Genesis** *By Betty Tracy*
- **Foundations of Faith** *By John J. Wiltse*
- **Galatians: A View From the Inside** *By Daniel R. Wiltse*
- **History Foretold: Daniel** *By Betty Tracy*
- **Homeschool: Why, What, How** *By Betty Tracy*
- **Rubies, Silk and Chocolate Covered Peanuts: Proverbs 31 and Titus 2** *By Betty Tracy*
- **The Family Unit** *By Betty Tracy*
- **Thy Word Have I Hidden** *By Betty Tracy*

Children's Books:
- **…And a Mommy** *By Betty Tracy*
- **So Sad** *By Betty Tracy*
- **Someday I'll Be a Daddy** *By Betty Wiltse*
- **The Luckiest One** *By Betty Tracy*
- **Why Am I Homeschooled?** *By Betty Tracy*

Pamphlets:
- **A Mother's Job** *By Betty Tracy*
- **Beginnings** *By Betty Tracy*
- **Courtship or Dating?** *By Betty Tracy*
- **Dear Family and Friends** *By Betty Tracy*
- **Do Babies Go To Heaven** *By Betty Tracy*
- **Examine Yourselves** *By Anonymous and John J Wiltse*
- **How to Read Music** *By Betty Tracy*
- **How to Teach the Bible** *By Betty Tracy*
- **Is There a God?** *By Betty Tracy*
- **Paul: Apostle or Apostate?** *By John J Wiltse*
- **Prayer** *By Betty Tracy*
- **Proper Manners for the American Child** *By Betty Tracy*
- **Raw Milk: A Real Food** *By Betty Tracy*
- **Satan is Not a Fallen Angel** *By Betty Tracy*
- **The Family Integrated Church** *By Betty Tracy*
- **What Meaneth This?** *By John J Wiltse*
- **Where Did We Come From?** *By Betty Tracy*
- **Which Mountain?** *By John J Wiltse*
- **Why King James?** *By Betty Tracy*

Contact thebettysbooks.com
or
Bread of Life Christian Fellowship
P.O. Box 20009
Carson City, Nevada, 89721

www.ingramcontent.com/pod-product-compliance
Lightning Source LLC
Chambersburg PA
CBHW051716040426
42446CB00008B/920